Biographies

YONNI I Tom Ross-Williams
Stage credits include: *After Orlando* (Fir
(Southwark Playhouse); *Negril Beach* (Bu.
(Chris Goode & Co); *Vieux Carré* (King's Head & We.
Dunsinane (RSC); *Shalom Baby* (Theatre Royal Stratford Ea..
(Kneehigh); *Amphibians* (Offstage) and *Prime Resident* (Soho). TV/r...
credits include: *Fit* (Peccadillo Films); *Free* (Team Angelica); *Forgotten
Man*, *The Grove* (RTÉ) and the short film *Dog* (LSFF).

Tom is also a campaigner and Artistic Director of the political theatre
company, Populace. His most recent show about toxic masculinity,
Give Me Your Skin (co-created with Oonagh Murphy), is being
produced by the Battersea Arts Centre for a premiere in summer 2017.

@tomrosswilliams

Director I Lucy Wray
Directing credits (inc. dramaturgy): *They Built It. No One Came.* by
Callum Cameron (Greenwich/UK tour/Pleasance, Edinburgh); *Left My
Desk at Crescent House* by Olivia Hirst (Litmus Fest/Pleasance
Islington); *Royal Vauxhall* by Desmond O'Connor (Underbelly,
Edinburgh); *Eggs* by Florence Keith Roach (VAULT Festival);
Goodstock by Olivia Hirst (Greenwich/New Diorama/Pleasance,
Edinburgh). As Dramaturg: *Give Me Your Skin* by Tom Ross Williams
and Oonagh Murphy (BAC/CPT).

She is Associate Director with METIS, Young Vic/New Wolsey) and
co-Artistic Director of Populace. Populace was set up in response to
anti-cuts protests in March 2011 and has performed work at the
Bush, West Yorkshire Playhouse, Theatre Royal Stratford East, Lyric
Hammersmith, Ovalhouse and Rich Mix.

@lucywray_

Writer I Stephen Laughton

Theatre credits include: *Screens* (Theatre503); *Run* (VAULT Festival; Southwark Playhouse); *Nine* (Arcola); *Marina Abramovic is Staring at Me* (Railroad Playhouse, NY; Cell Theatre, NYC).

TV credits include: *Black Hill* (Lime Pictures); *Forward* (Blacklisted Films); *Tumble* (Double M Films).

Film credits include: *The Hobby* (Blacklisted Films); *RWD/FWD* (Fully Focussed/GOOD Agency/Restorative Justice Council; nominated for a Drum Content and Charity Film Award).

Stephen has produced a range of critically acclaimed film, theatre and TV productions: projects including the Academy Award shortlisted *Unknown White Male* and multi-award-winning *Tottenham Ayatollah*. Stephen co-directed a short-film *Recompense*, which screened at the BFI and was an official selection for the New York Independent Film Festival, where it won Best Actor, Best Actress and Best Directorial Debut in the Short Film Category.

Stephen is the Creative Director of iN BLOOM.

@STEPHENLAUGHT0N

Press and Publicity I Paul Bloomfield

With over ten years of experience in theatre production and direction, public relations and social media, and strong media connection in specialised outlets including the Jewish press, LGBT media and theatre news; Paul has worked for large brands across a spectrum of vertical sectors. Consumer brands include Horlicks and Radox, entertainment and leisure projects include Mr Gay UK and the launch of the London 2012 Cycling Centre – Lee Valley VeloPark.

Paul is the Executive Director of iN BLOOM

@BloomyP

Stage Manager I Lil Davis

Lil started working in stage management and lighting whilst studying at Cygnet Training Theatre. Since then she has been working in theatres both in Israel and UK in a wide range of roles, from stage manager and assistant director to performer, lighting designer and translator.

Credits include: All-Male *HMS Pinafore* (national tour); *Thought to Flesh* (VAULT Festival); *The Farmer's Wife* (New Theatre, Exeter); *Pericles, The Merchant of Venice* (Cambridge Shakespeare Festival); *The Flies, In The Last Act* (Karov Theatre, Israel); *Marat/Sade, The Crucible* (Nissan Nativ Acting Studio, Israel); *Raggabones&House* (Peregrine Ensemble); *Miguel, I Am Sofia* (Tristan Bates/Canal Café).

Lil is co-founder of multicultural theatre company Peregrine Ensemble.

@msLilDavis

Composer I Helen Sartory

Helen is a former classical musician, Helen has been developing the first immersive electronic music experience, ADRODES for VAULT 2017.

Her credits include *Run* (VAULT Festival/Southwark Playhouse); *Androdes* (VAULT Festival/UK tour); *Exposure* (short film).

@iamSARTORY

Sound Designer I Anna Clock

Anna Clock is a London-based sound designer, composer and cellist with a special interest in interdisciplinary collaboration, challenging audience/performer relationships and headphone space in theatre and film. Recent work in theatre includes: *Graphene: Wonder Materials//Tape Piece* (created with Sarah Rowland Hill as part of a Brighter Sound residency with Anna Meredith at the Museum of Science and Industry, Manchester); *Constellations* (The Cockpit, London); *In Utero* (Very Clock – commissioned by the ICC, Dublin); *The Timestealers* (Very Clock – London); *Laughing Matter* (End of Moving Walkway – The King's Head, London); *One Moment* (Very Clock, premiered at the Roundhouse Camden as part of *We Are Now* festival); *Poke in the Eye* (Georgie Morrell – Edinburgh Fringe); *Boobies* (Very Clock – Styx, Celebration of International Women's Day); *Snail Walk* (Discotheque Collective – site-specific locations in Dublin/Berlin).

@annaclock

Lee Gould I Production Designer

Lee Gould is a freelance animator, illustrator and artist working across the creative industries in print, web, television, computer games and music videos. He has worked with the BBC, the *Guardian*, Yahoo, EA games and Lloyds TSB.

Projects/campaigns include: Opening Lines (Guardian), Breakfast muffins (Dorset Cereals), Mirror's Edge (EA Games), Britain's Best Architecture (Guardian), When Beauty Goes Wrong (BBC), Britain's Biggest Breakfast (Cancer Research), Sunsmart (Nivea) Pip and Nut Cookbook (Pip and Nut).

@LeeBenGould

Lucy Hansom I Lighting Designer

Lucy trained at Central St Martins in Theatre Design, specialising in Lighting Design and Scenography for Dance, and subsequently at Laban. She joined the technical theatre staff at The Place in 2007 and combined this with commissions for designs, including for Slung Low at the Barbican and James Wilton Dance at Sadler's Wells. Now freelance, other notable designs include *A Night with Boy Blue Entertainment* at the Barbican Main House Theatre and the Matthew Bourne NACA showcase for John Ross at Hackney Empire. In 2014 Lucy collaborated as lighting designer with Michael Mannion on *Athletes* by Riccardo Buscarini, which won the Place Prize for Dance.

Lucy is the resident lighting designer for LCDS's postgraduate performance company as well as for Just Us Dance Theatre.

Kieron Johnson I Lighting Assistant

Kieron Johnson is a freelance Lighting Designer and Production Manager, specialising in Lighting for Theatre, Contemporary Dance and Live Performance Art. An Affiliate Member of the Association of Lighting Designers, he has worked alongside many institutions, choreographers and companies including Trinity Laban Conservatoire of Music and Dance, The Place, Kerry Nicholls, Transitions Dance Company, Edge Dance Company, Company Wayne McGregor, Matthew Bourne for New Adventures, Opera North, Jessica Wright, Stephanie Schober, Dam Van Huynh and Motionhouse.

Upcoming designs include *Thirst* (The Space), *You're Human Like The Rest of Them* (Finborough); *Phroot Salad* (Lyric Hammersmith); *Gulliver's Travels* (Alexandra).

@KieronJohnsonLD

iN BLOOM

iN BLOOM is a boutique production and public relations company who specialise in theatre, film and cabaret.

As producers we bring with us more than ten years of working across a range of acclaimed and award-winning film, TV and theatre productions. Our projects have appeared at the Bradford Playhouse, VAULT Festival, Leeds Pride, Theatre503, The Roundhouse, The Viaduct Showbar, Southwark Playhouse, Leeds City Hall, The Carriageworks, The Royal Vauxhall Tavern and Bar Broadway, Brighton. We've worked with theatres including the Royal Court, Hampstead, Headlong and the Young Vic. Film and TV projects have been released across the mainstream UK channels, for international theatrical cinematic release, the BFI and have won spots at film festivals including Cannes, Sundance, Berlin, New York, Sydney and London. Award recognition include wins at the BAFTAS, RTS, Sundance and New York Film Festivals. We've also been shortlisted for an Academy Award.

Our PR clients include the BBC, Liberal Judaism, LJS, BKY, Little Green Man Nursery, Ash Healthcare and Janbarree Ltd. Agency work has included Mother, J Walter Thompson, Blue Rubicon, The Lounge Group and Engine.

@in_bloom_ent
inbloomentertainment.co.uk

THE NEW POSTCODE FOR JEWISH LIFE

JW3 is a state-of-the-art community and cultural venue in West Hampstead, a charity established for the benefit of the Jewish community, the local community, and for the people of London. Designed by Lifschutz Davidson Sandilands, JW3 houses a 270-seat auditorium, a 60-seat cinema, a demonstration kitchen, dance studios, classrooms and Zest, JW3's in-house restaurant and bar.

www.jw3.org.uk

A playground for Ambitious Artists to create work for Adventurous Audiences

The Bunker is a new Off-West End theatre in London Bridge housed in a former underground parking garage. The space has been transformed from its original abandoned state into a unique 110-seater deep beneath the pavements of Southwark Street.

With four concrete pillars marking out the thrust performance space, an eclectic mix of audience seating on three sides of the stage, and a snug bar tucked into the corner of the venue, The Bunker has a unique character that feels both classical and contemporary.

Founded by Artistic Director Joshua McTaggart and Executive Producer Joel Fisher, The Bunker's first season of work opened in October 2016 with *Skin A Cat* by Isley Lynn, an award-winning transfer from VAULT Festival. The Bunker puts artists at the centre of its programming, and the space functions as a gallery as well as a performance space.

Driven by a desire to create theatre that is an event for its audience, The Bunker is attempting to redefine what an evening at the theatre is like. From post-show poetry to pop-up dance performances, from scratch nights to movie nights, there is always something different on offer at The Bunker, but the focus is always the same: An unforgettable evening of entertainment, discovery, and adventure.

Find Out More
You can find out more about The Bunker, our first season, and our other work by visiting our website, calling the box office, or dropping us an email.

Website: www.bunkertheatre.com
Box Office: 0207 234 0486
Email: info@bunkertheatre.com
Address: 53a Southwark Street, London, SE1 1RU

The Bunker Team

Artistic Director	Joshua McTaggart
Executive Producer	Joel Fisher
Associate Director	Sara Joyce
Technical Manager	Hannah Fisher
Bar Manager	Lee Whitelock

The Bunker could not run smoothly without the incredible work of our volunteer ushers. If you would like to join The Bunker team, then email us on **info@bunkertheatre.com**

Our Supporters

The Bunker would like to thank the following individuals for their support in getting The Bunker off the ground and helping us to launch our first season of work:

Philip and Chris Carne, Laurence Isaacson, The Edwin Fox Foundation, Mark Schnebli, Monty Fisher, Charlotte Houghteling, Joscelyn Fox and Lt Cdr Paul Fletcher, Roger Horrell, Melvyn Dubbell, Quay Chu, Paul Slawson-Price. George Arthur, Roger Horrell, Sara Naudi, Felicity Trew, Edward Glover, Matthew Payne, Alex Leung, Barbara Cantelo. The Stephen Sondheim Society, Matt Brinkler, Max Stafford-Clark.

As a registered Community Interest Company (Company Number 10330447) that does not receive subsidy, The Bunker relies on generous support from individuals, foundations, and companies to help us make relevant and ambitious theatre. If you would like to support the work that The Bunker creates, you can find out how at

www.bunkertheatre.com/support-us

Acknowledgements

There are so many people to thank! And that's kind of amazing – because all of the support we have had is incredible.

First up, Oli and Lauren – although I missed you on this – it still really felt like you were here. We wouldn't have gotten this far without you, and you'll always be part of the *Run* family. Thank you so much for everything you've done for us and all your hard work. This one is for you. Peter and Heather, I'm sorry too that you couldn't join us this time but thanks for helping us get back up to speed again! The additions to the team have felt like extending the family, which is quite lovely. Lucy, it's no mean feat coming into a show that's already been up before – thanks, lovely. You've done a cracking job. I couldn't be happier. Tom. Just wow. You're incredible. The rest of the team – Lighting Lucy, Lee, Anna, Lil, Michelle, Helen and Kieron – you're all so talented and awesome and it's been great having you aboard. You're amazing. Thank you! Ryan Forde Iosco, Lauren Brown and James Huntrods deserve a big THANK YOU for the original Courting Drama platform that started all this. Matt and Sarah Liisa at Nick Hern Books for being cool about deadlines and typos. Twice.

To all the donors, patrons and supporters – wow! You've been incredible. Jan – you're an actual angel – thank you. Barry and Mark – cheers for all the help with spaces and that. To all of my panellists – thank you so much for joining in. It's been so much fun. John – sorry I couldn't have done this with you, man. Next time. My fellow Playdaters – Dave Ralf, Isley Lynn, Chris Adams, Poppy Corbett, Vinay Patel and Sarah Kosar – I don't think I could do this without you. I certainly wouldn't want to. You're all so inspiring, talented and clever. I walk in the shadow of giants. Whilst we're talking about my peers – John O'Donovan, Nathan Lucky Wood, Adam Hughes, Amanda Castro, Sam Potter, Milly Thomas, Joshua St. Johnson, Camilla Whitehill and Sarah Meadows – I freaking love what you do, it both excites me and keeps me on my toes. My lovely agent Nick, and of course Laura – just thank you. Marcus Markou and Sophie Mitchell – it's a pleasure playing at telly with you and I can't thank you enough for enabling my nonsense. David Chikwe for sticking with… You're so lovely and loyal… Sue Teddern for keeping me off social media when I'm trying to skive. To the Marlborough team and especially Ema – thanks for everything. JW3 have been so supportive, I can't thank you enough. Sarah Sigal is my personal hero. Just thank you. The Bunker Team – Sara, Hannah and Lee – this has been super fun. Cheers for being so on board. Joel and Josh. Legends. Thanks, boys.

It has become increasingly clear, especially over the last year, that I have the best friends in the universe – Sam Hayes, Lee Gould, Sara Marti, Mandy Owen, Rachel Vere, Dave the girl Ghaly, Stephanie Bratnick, Toni Butler,

Amy Carrick – thank you for putting up with me and my nonsense. I love you guys. Ella Hoskin, Raul Fuertes, Nick Hoare, Guesty, Rosie R-B, Paul Cartwright, Stu Withers, Vega, Mike Hartley, Jess Snell, Tina Barnes, Emma Powers, Katherina Lokenhagen, Dave H, Div, Luke Mably, Jimmy Bradshaw, Caron Copek, Gem and Andrew, Jade Martin, Katie Metcalfe, Shane Lawlor, Sophie Barison, Paul Green, Emma De Wet, Jamie Mulligan, Emma Schimminger, Jon Mcleod, Cass Adamson, Joseph Baker, Leah Henry, Zoe Lawrence, Enma Ong – you're some of the greatest people I know, I don't see you enough, but you're always there. To the team at LJ but especially Danny Rich, Shelley Shocolinsky-Dwyer, Charley Baginsky, Sandra Kviat and Simon Rothstein – thank you for looking out for me. Words can't express.

To Rachel Benjamin, Rene Pfertzel, Alex Wright, Phillipa Rubin and Alex Weiss at LJS. Similarly, thanks for the love, support and care. Gemma Trippas, Rob Delijani, Izzy and Matthew Benjamin-Davies, Sadie Struss and Daniel Gibson, Max Gelman and Alice Piterova, Alan Parmeter and Samantha Cozens. Genuinely – I love you guys. The LJS young adult dinner group… you're so wonderful and supportive. Thank you.

Max Lewis is a genuine superhero.

Fiona Leckerman is incredibly special. Thank you for turning up and sticking around.

And Paul, although I can't believe that my Hebrew has gotten worse… You were supposed to be all over that. I love you.

S.L.

RUN

Stephen Laughton

'Remember the Sabbath day, keep it holy'

Exodus, 20

Character

YONNI, *seventeen*

It's chaos in the kitchen.

Yelling. Clatter… shit boiling over.

Washing
Spinning…

A dog barking. We don't even have a dog.

Like it's brown.
About yay big.
Yappy.
Keeps looking at me.

I'm worried it's hungry.

But it's mainly jumping around my little brother Jesse, who's grinning like a moron and mirroring the stupid thing.

And it's the happiest I've seen him in months.
Which I guess is good.

And Devorah, my mother, pipes up from her prep every now and then.
Kinda absently telling them to shut up.

I lean down, rub the dog's head, kind of warily.

Devorah proffers a *hi love,* asks about the day
There's something too kind in her smile…

And the dog stares back.
With that look…
Head to one side… cocked…
It looks cute but basically means *I wanna eat ya.*

We're not allowed pets cos of my allergies apparently, and I can't imagine a world where Devorah would even allow it in her kitchen. I'm not sure it's kosher enough.

And it's adding to this sense of chaos and because tensions already feel high today, and I've got this slow creeping anxiety tightening across my chest, I'm mainly too scared to ask why it's here...

Jesse's having fun though.
Which from an IQ standpoint makes sense. And it's nice the way my little bro seriously just found himself a soulmate. He's making some kind of Scooby Dooby 'yes he is' kind of noise at it. And basically looks a bit 'smesh'.

It's Friday.

March.

About 4 p.m.

The weekly pre-Shabbat panic is officially in full swing. Devorah is frantically cracking individual eggs into a small clear glass. She holds it up to the light. Scans to the right, spins to the left. Lowers the glass to see it from above and then lifts back up to check below.

Satisfied with her inspection she tips the egg into her left hand. And oozes the yolk back to her right.
Then left.
To her right.
And back...

The white of the egg drip-dripping into the bowl below.

She cracks and repeats.

Cracks.
And repeats.

Orders me to chop carrots and I begrudgingly begin.
Soon working out that Jesse's in shit again.

Devorah's berating him over this week's misdemeanours – including the dog... Knew it. And something about detention... again... and his general backchatting-attitude shit.

And there's barking and jumping and chopping and cracking and Jesse's jigging about the place. And answering back. Thinking it's all a bit funny.

And it builds and it builds and it builds and it –
Stop.

I fucking hate carrots.
Seriously like proper repulsed.
And she knows it.

They look gross. Orange actually offends me. And you
cannot… *seriously* cannot… boil a carrot without it festering
everything it touches with its limpity carroty bollocks.
They ruin.
Everything.

No one wants to eat your irritation, my darling…
That sweet sweet smile again.

Well don't make me chop the fucking carrots then.
Don't say that.
Obvs.

Just tut, and…

Breathe.

And on my in-breath Devorah lets out an exasperated *oy* as she
empties another eggy glass into the waste-disposal-unit thing…

Blood spot.
On the yolk.

She grabs a fresh glass. Stacking up the tainted, sullied glasses
next to the sink.

And as she places it, the dog knocks into her and she lets rip
at Jesse. She won't tell him again. *Get that thing out of the
kitchen.*

And then back to beating the shit out of the egg whites.

Reuben, my father, walks in. He drops a bottle of Kiddush wine
on the counter.

Grunts.

Leaves. He's fun like that.

Devorah doesn't notice.
I don't think she notices him at all any more.
It's like they somehow just exist in spite of each other these days.

In apsis. *Apsides*.
Aphelion.
Apart.

I can't remember when I last saw them talk.

Whites now mixed I can't help but pick up the rhythm... I can
feel it in my chest as she slaps in the matzo and starts forming
the dumplings.
I put the knife down.
I need to just –

Breathe.

It's Bedlam.

About one forty-five.

Another Friday, shit... nearly two years ago now and lunch is
nearly done.
Teachers sweep in periphery, and we're all in huddles...

It's muck-up day today...
And the Year 11s, me and mine, get to bolt after next period...

Study leave.

Or as we like to call it 'getting stoned with your mates all week
then fully cramming with the geeky kids you've hung shit on
for the last four years the night of your modular science exam'.

Then passing.

And there's buzzing and manoeuvring and rowdiness in the air.

The kids in my year all excited 'bout egg and flour and maybe
the odd firework. Some kid trying to convince us to catapult
chickens at the school walls.

I hope they're kosher.

And in the rabble I spot you.

Smiling, cool, somewhat removed…

Soaking it up…

Like, the day after we met, like properly… At that bus stop…

And you're standing there.…

Like. Grinning…
Like that.

Hot.

Blue-green eyes.
Messy hair. Cute smile.

You're fair.
Not like me.
Intellectual. Less like me.
A nice Ashkenazi boy.

You're deep. Literal… Something of the artist…
Bit more like me…

Watching it all unfold.

Then you spot me.
Nod.
And I freeze.

Eyes locked.

One…
Two…

And I brave it.

Walk over.

Leave my mates behind as they head off for whatever little
juvenile ploy they'll play…

Then it's us. Alone.

Hey. You say.

And it's fully disarming.
Kinda calming.

But before we even get to say another thing I look up and there she is.

Devorah.

Raging.

In the middle of the playground.
Dragging Jesse behind her...

And I freeze and she's instantly all over me ordering that we leave and I'm like *NO* no way *it's my last day* but she's having none of it she's not coming back and I'm telling her I can make my own way home and everyone's watching and she's like don't answer back and everyone's watching and she tells me we're leaving and before I can argue and everyone's watching I'm warned that I better not start as well.

And everyone's watching.

And I'm horrified.

And we lock eyes, you and I, and you mouth to me... ask me if I'm alright.

And the whole thing seems to swim...

As everyone's watching.

And in the –

Shame.
That rises.
The the the panic... that rises...

You hold me.
With your gaze.

And as as as I'm lead away....

Head down... whispering frantically to Devorah about how embarrassing she is, not really paying attention to her total eppy about her meeting with the Head and Jesse and his Hebrew teacher Mr Weiner and how Reuben is probably gonna go batshit crazy –

You catch up.

Pull me back for a second and I'm torn between you and
Devorah, glance back at her as you pull out a pen… start to
write on my arm… I guess it's muck-up day, so it's kinda what
you do and she's calling me back and I pull away.

Smile. Apologetically.

Clock what you've written.

And exhale.
Realise I've been holding my breath.

Adam.
07590 –
And I commit it to –

Stop.

And blur.

Later.

As Reuben rages. Jesse is sullen.
Devorah looks between… her perception, her focus, her interest
conflicted.

Afflicted.

She appeals to Reuben's sense of reason.
But that's long gone and the word suspended rattles around
the room.

SUSPENDED.

With such force that it threatens to bring down the foundations.

Suspended…

Which is kinda what it does to the room.

Suspended.

And I sit and I stare, like not entirely sure why I have to be here
but soon find myself completely embodied within this entirely
fucked-up scene…

And looking back I find myself almost agreeing with Reuben's fervent polemic... that maybe it was the mood of the summer itself taking a stranglehold on our family and that maybe it created the catalyst to the long slow implosion of our absolute entirety... maybe those rising tensions over war in Gaza and all the shit in this city, all the 'Sieg Heil' salutes and the security at school and the swastikas on street signs and the name-calling on Facebook and Twitter and the windows smashed at that synagogue in Belfast and that Rabbi attacked in Gateshead and the mutilation of that Israeli lady in Colindale did indeed make it just super fucking shit to be a Jew in pretty much any British city the summer before last and maybe that fear and and and and that frustration found itself projected...

Infected.
Directed.
Home.

And maybe that's what caused my little brother to go batshit crazy that day cos Mr Weiner was really living up to his name...

And maybe that's what's sending my ridiculous little yampy fuck of a father, with his totally embodied small-dog-syndrome bullshit even more crazy today and fuelling this total overreaction And maybe that's why Devorah finally explodes.

And *fuck* does she...

And Jesse sobs and Devorah cries and Reuben thunders.

And then she slaps him.

And I'm completely stunned. Shocked into silence.

Because *Reuben*... Reuben slaps her back.

And she doesn't retaliate. No.

The ear-splitting silence is enough.

She takes Jesse's hand. And crosses the room.
Reuben's mumbled apology lost in the gulf.

She reaches the door and barks my name.

Yonni...

Like it's an order.

Yonni.

And we all just stand there…

I'm Devorah's boy all over… 'cept I'm a better cook.
Kinda have to be.

Like I'm really particular about my roast potatoes. And as I go
back into the kitchen I clock Devorah basting like a maniac –
I say basting… she's shovelling litres of…
I mean.
She's essentially deep-frying them right.
In the oven.
And I have to find a way to save them because I'm not sure my
stomach can handle all that schmaltz today.

I don't think I can really handle much. If I'm honest.

I ask if she's going Carmelli's. To pick up the challah.
She counters that I could go to Carmelli's.
I offer that if she's getting beigels too, she might need the car.
She questions the amount of beigels I think we need.
I point out that we all like beigels very much.
She requests that I quite literally get on my bike and go fetch
challah and beigels.
She also suggest I might want to stop being a smart-arse.
I remind her that she has another son, with a dog now, who
might need a walk…

She stares.
Head to one side… cocked…

Go to Carmelli's, Yonni.

And she pauses for effect.
Don't make me ask you again.

And that's my potatoes fucked.

I walk round to the garage. Jump on my bike.
I've still got your stickers all over the seat, the ones from
Jew camp.

And I'm cycling down the Queens Road and I think about how excited I was when I found out you were going.

Like, I nearly couldn't be arsed. I've been doing LJY-Netzer shit since I was like... I dunno, like ten...

And I didn't even know you were into the whole youth-movement thing... let alone thinking about Hadracha.
And it makes sense you know. You'd make a great youth leader.
And I grin... I'm excited and I start making lists and spreadsheets of the shit I need to buy and

Stop.

First. Day. Blur.

And whether it's the luck of the draw or a little behind-the-scenes fudging it turns out I'm in your dorm.

And your bunk is next to mine.

And all the arriving plus the intro stuff multiplied by the dinner divided by the benching to the power of the songs equal a really long fucker of a day.

I crawl into bed.
Exhausted.

Pull the blanket up and notice I'm reciting the angel prayer in my head.

Beshaym Adonai Elohay Yisra'el
Mimini Micha'el
Umismali Gavri'el
Umil'fanei Uri'el
Umayacharei Refa'el
Ve'al roshi Shechinat El.

I dunno why...

Just enjoy...
How...
How lovely it is...

How safe it always makes me feel.

GCSEs are over.
Summer's here…
And I dunno.

Cos I've got the wall to my right.
And you to my left.
My own Michael. My own Gabriel.
And maybe, for now I don't even need Uriel or Raphael.
Maybe I feel actually safe.
Actually.
Happy.
Protected.

And safe.

I've turned slowly on to my left side and I face you.

You're even more beautiful in sleep.

The room glows an eerie green from the fire escape and
I synchronise my breath to yours and on your in-breath
I breathe in and on your out-breath I breathe out.

I will you to turn over.

To smile at me.

But soon fall into deep dead sleep and lost somewhere in the
twilight of my thoughts, I dream of blue, and time itself hustles
and hastens in the gloom and in no time at all I blur into waking
and you're there.

Smiling.

Stop.

I've overslept, and you didn't want to wake me.

I smile back at you.

Stop.
Wish I could take a picture.
But you tell me to get up… there's loads to do today…
And I look at you. At beautiful beautiful you.

And I jump out of bed and I catch the smirk in the sideways
glance, the way your eyes pass quickly over me.

And that look gets me through the blur of the day.

And…

Later.

Everyone has gone to bed… I'm reading about the fall of the
Austro-Hungarian Empire and you tap me on the shoulder…
tell me to shut the fuck up before I've even said a word and you
gesture out.
To the garden.
I follow in silence.

Pass the tennis courts.
The weird knobbly-tree thing.
The toady-pondy-bridge thing.

And I'm soon transfixed.
On your fingers –
– as you slowly roll the joint.

I'm I'm I'm.
Enchanted.
By… by –

By the delicacy.
Dexterity.
The intricacy of the movement.

And before I know it you've sparked up and you pass on and
I draw in
And the THC hits me as you land on Venus.

Because if you were an alien, or or or or from any other planet
you'd be from Venus…

That feels right, it goes with your eyes.

And I ask why, ask *what's so cool about Venus* and you tell me
how it rotates anti-clockwise.

And how the atmospheric pressure of Venus is ninety-two times
greater than Earth's.

Geek.

And that makes sense to you… in your head… cos that's
sometimes how it feels sometimes…

Like overwhelming I guess and the way you make yourself so
vulnerable to me.

By telling me that –

– and the way your brow furrows and your stubble bristles and
your eyes tear a bit make me fully realise that –

Stop.

You explain how Venus is the hottest planet in the Solar System
which totally makes sense cos you're like seriously smoking…

And it's the second-brightest object in the night sky.
Of course it is.

You're luminous.

Then you ask what planet I'm from?
And I'm nowhere near as articulate or philosophical or actually
as geeky as you are.

So you suggest that I'm from Ganymede.

There's water on Ganymede.
Deep, deep down below the surface.
And you reckon it's warm.

And you tell me how Ganymede radiates Aurora, and that it has
oxygen, like there's not enough for us to breathe, but it's
oxygen nonetheless…

And that's pretty fucken cool, no?
And your whole shtick just… makes me –

Stop.

We're in another dorm. A mess of clothes and books and shower
gel and just boy-stuff entangle and sprawl on the bunks below.
I'm wired. Paranoid. Kinda cold.

We've smoked weed at the end of the tennis court again.
Creep back into the house…
It's haunted
I grin at you as I'm brushing my teeth.
As you're telling me about some fucked-up murdering-vicar dude.
And that's what you get, I pipe up, when you base a religious
system on original sin.
And you nod.
Very good, you say.

And you brush past me as you walk into the toilet.

It's gentle. Accidental.
Fully kinda mental.

And we both clock it.

And quick as a flash you're back.
Brushing your teeth too.
Grinning again as you blatantly steal my toothpaste.
You've never used the whitening before.
Your mom always buys the sensitive stuff.
Less abrasive.

And I steal these glances

In the mirror…

…and I don't know where to put them.
What they mean.

We spit at the same time.

Our hands brush and suddenly you take it…
I think you do. Maybe I do. I don't know cos the world has
stopped and your look asks me if it's okay

And it is oh my god it's okay it's like so okay so just please just
do it just like please just do it just please.

And time itself feels like it's been affected by the weight of this.

And lips almost touch
And I inhale you.
And my heart stops.

And my world stops.
And my

     everything

          just stops.

And we kiss.

               ...backwards turns world the and

                fuck
                  I
               don't
               even
               know
              which
               way

And
Everything.
Deep in me.

Just...

Stop.

Austria. You creep into my bunk... Wake me up with a kiss.
Pull me close.
Are you gonna sleep here...?
But you can't... and it makes you sad. It makes me sad.
It's so hot up here you say.
And I'm proud of my reply. I been studying my science...
Well... Wikipedia.
That's because heat rises.

Well why is space so cold then? Eh? Tell me that, brains…?
And you're so pleased with yourself cos you out-scienced me.
Again.
And it's so cute that I don't want to tell you that.

And we spoon, kiss, chat and soon too soon fall asleep.
Until we're awakened.

And my pleas and my panic are lost in the accusation, lost in
the punishment as we're kicked off camp and you're given
some kind of warning.

I always order in Hebrew at Carmelli's.

I've been doing it since I was like six.

The woman in there, Mrs Carmelli, has pretty much watched
me grow up and week on week we run through our little *how
are you* exchange. She's too busy and can't wait for Shabbat,
I either love or hate school…
And can't wait for Shabbat.

Sh'tayim challot v'tesha'beigelim be'vaka'shah.

She busies about sorting it.

I work out that I'm probably not gonna eat much tonight so
I should fill up now.

I'm tempted by cream cheese and lox.
I check out the pastries.
Gam ahat bourek'ah.
Tah'poo'ahkh ah'dah'mah.

We banter more.

There's this look she gives me, that seems to penetrate my
everything as she asks me in English if today has been okay.

I nod. Quickly. Look down. Quickly.

And pay. Quickly.

Leave on a *todah* and as I cycle back down Golders Green
Road...

...I fall deeper into your orbit.

Venus pulling Ganymede, closer to the warming sun.

Though it's freezing in the bedroom.

I'm close, close I'm closer still
And feel your warmth as we bunch in...
You're wearing shorts?
It's freezing.
It's summer.
Your house is really cold.
I think you're just scared.
I affirm that yes I could potentially be freaking the fuck out.
And you assure me that it's okay.
We're just gonna kiss and spoon and nothing's gonna happen.
Then you grin.
Unless you want it to.
And although I do... nothing happens.

Because we want it to be right.

We want it to be conscious.
Well that's what you said and although I don't quite get it,
I certainly don't wanna be unconscious. Right?

And we kiss and we slowly fall asleep, feet, legs and arms
entwined.

And later.

And I wake in the night with a start, and gently uncurl myself
from you and I head out into the labyrinth in urgent search of
the loo.

And I'm super-tired and can't be arsed to lift the lid so piss into
the sink, absently make a note that I probably need to drink more
water... at least lay off the coffee and and and suddenly like
fucking fuckety fuck like fully horror of horrors as a precariously

balanced toothbrush tumbles right into the jet stream and FUCK.
So gross.

I wash it.
Twice.

With soap.
Twice.

And I come back to the room and you've moved in the bed and
you're naked, and although I knew you were naked, I felt you
were naked, I just didn't expect to see you actually naked and
I crawl into you and it's still so cold and we sleepily kiss until
you wake and it suddenly suddenly feels right and we're
tangled and knotted and fully submerged...

And as we tumble through space in this new co-orbital
configuration an axis somewhere shifts and it kick-starts a series
of aftershocks that fundamentally change everything.

Devorah's burnt the chicken. Knob.

And she's literally flapping around like a psychopath as the
pre-Shabbat panic turns into full-on freaking the fuck out as
she starts wittering about defrosting salmons in the fridge and
could she do them instead and have the chicken for lunch
tomorrow after shul but there's not enough and I tell her no one
actually gives a shit really and she tells me off for my language
and I instantly get over-defensive and shout right back cos *I'm
just trying to help alright*.

And you can tell I've hit a nerve... but she's being patient
with me.

Too too kindly tells me it's okay.
Too too kindly asks if I want to go relax.

I hate it when they're being patient with me.

Hot spray hits me and I gasp.

Step closer into the stream. Close my eyes. Wash my hair.
But I don't scrub too hard.
I won't wash you away.

And I think about the first time you clocked me in the shower.
As I turned round you were standing there. Watching me…

Saying I look fit.
That you've got something to show me…

Oh yeah, I say…

On the iPad. A whale has been washed up on Dungeness Beach.
It's been there all night and it could die and you wanna do
something we should do something.

And you tell me how they can explode.

That in the process of decomposition, methane and other gases
accumulate in the body and and the build-up of pressure, plus
the disintegration of the whale's flesh, potentially causes the
whole thing to burst.

It's cute when you get excited about telling me stuff.
You ask me what I think.

I hope they can save it.

You explain, slowly, cos I'm a dumbass that your parents are
back tomorrow and that you want one last adventure before life
starts again…

Sea blurs sky blur as the wash blurs the wind and this isolated
milieu against this desolate headland that's dominated by these
two massive power stations is bare and bleak and wild and
windswept and just so so so hauntingly beautiful.

We walk slowly down the long long boardwalk.

Wrapped in empty eeriness around us.

Dungeness is Britain's only desert and the beach shelves
sharply and the currents seems strong.

The coast feels rugged.

The sky feels vacant.

I'm mesmerised as we walk across pebbles and shingle and
watch the waves crash on to the beach.

Flotsam washes up and around whilst ubiquitous junk and jetsam seem to whisper their own memories and history.

Then suddenly you take my hand, start singing Leonard Cohen at me, spinning me up and around, here and about... .

First dance at our wedding you declare...
Really?
You shrug.
You've thought that far ahead?
Say maybe it's me that's been thinking that far ahead...
But you're the one who's really into Cohen.
You agree that yeah you are. As you carry on singing at me.

In the voice.

He sings a few lines of 'Dance Me to the End of Love' by Leonard Cohen.

And you spin me under your arms and you whisper the sweet beginnings of our own memories as I twist back out and you pull me face to face, kiss, send me spinning off –

And then we spot it.

And then we stop.

She's small, around twenty-two feet.
You reckon she's probably a young humpback.

You start telling me how they're known for their magical songs but that noise pollution is the sea is really problematic and one of the main causes of beaching... and how the only day on record when whales' stress hormones noticeably decreased was in 2001, the day after 9/11 – the day when noise and ship traffic subsided. Because across the world... Hundreds and thousands of ships were confined to port.

And on that day, for the first time, in –
I don't even know how long...
The whales could finally hear one another.

On that beautiful day they could talk to one another.
Sing and shout and call to one another.

And most of the crowds have dispersed.
There's a couple of dog-walkers and some kids running about.

But it's mid-afternoon and the novelty factor is waning along
with the hope and people have shit to do like make dinner and
do their washing and live their inconsequential little lives and
I can't take my eyes off the dying magnificent beast.

You ask someone what's happening.
The quick response is nothing.
The slightly longer one is that we have to wait for the water
to rise.

And you check for the next high tide… and it's like five hours
away.
And the whale is dying.

And it looks hopeless, and it doesn't feel right to leave her to the
crabs and the wind, and it feels like we have to stay with her.

So we do.

And we spend ages on the beach trying to find some kind of
container and when we do, we spend the next few hours
pouring water all over her.

Just the three of us.
Me. And you. And Sophie the Humpback Whale.

That we met on Dungeness Beach. And we tell her we're really
chuffed that she's hanging out with us and we promise her that
we'll do our best to get her home.

I sit next to Sophie, she's leaning to her left and her right eye is
open, staring skyward. Her lower jaw is open too and I notice the
long filtering plates. You grin at me. They're called baleen plates.

Of course you'd know that.

Baleen.

And as I look into her eye, an eye that's as big as my fist, I see
my own reflection.
And maybe in that deep dark orb I also see fear.

And we have to do something.

And within forty-five minutes we have maybe ten, maybe like
maybe twelve people and we've dug a small trench and we start
to heave...
And it takes us a further thirty minutes to get anywhere.
But we do.
We get there.

We start to move the whale.

And... and it's hard and feels hopeless and panic rises and I can
see it rising in Sophie too and I hope she can understand, I hope
she gets that we're trying to help her but there's also a sense of
calm in her so maybe she does.

Maybe she gets it.

And as a group we push and we roll and we thrust her back out
into the sea.

And we make it.
We actually make it.

I'm not a great swimmer but I get her to a depth where she can
move... a depth that's maybe out of my depth and and as as as
exhausted as she is... as weak as she is...

She swims.

And before we lose our connection for ever, I take one last look
at her and as she looks back at me and I'm almost positive that
I see gratitude.

And then she's gone.
For ever.

It's rowdy round the table.

Lights. Candles. Family. Shouts.

Reuben... mixes grape juice with the wine for Kiddush.
He pours it out...

Takes the cup in his right hand, passes it to his left, and lowers
it back on to the palm of his open, outstretched right hand.
Holds it there...

Still
Steady.
Approximately, no, exactly nine inches above the table throughout

Unmoving.

Ba-ruch a-tah, A-do-nai he says
E-lo-hei-nu me-lech ha-o-lam he says
bo-rei p'ri ha-ga-fen he says

Amein we say
L'chaim we say

I try to say.
Because I struggle.

Food's gross.
Conversation's hard.
And these people are harder.

Granny repeats. Uncle and Reuben bicker.

And I feel drowsy, drowsier… like I haven't slept in days.
I haven't slept in a year and the slow creep digestive sleep
claws its way up from the inside out.

And I lose myself. And everyone around the table.

And I stare at you.
Just.
Stare.

And when I finally pull my gaze away… already… we're
benching…

Reuben chants and Devorah and my uncle and Granny and
Jesse and and I just want today to end.

Uncle asks about college. I nod. Smile. Try to –
My parents discuss a party down the street, pre-bar mitzvah
thing, we should go to.

Try to excuse myself. Say I'm tired. Can I go to bed please?
Another warning look from Reuben. I should help with dishes.
But Devorah tells me it's fine. I do look tired…

I'm wired, bent double. Hunched under the duvet that serves to block the twisted nematic light-modulated crystals that glow from my iPad. Because Devorah thinks turning off the wifi is some kind of no-tech-on-Shabbat deterrent because Devorah doesn't quite understand the concept of 4G or a data package.

And as I hide away in my little man-made blanket booth, I pretend like it's Tishrei... like I'm in my own tiny sukkah, like I get to tune in to my own tiny world in my own tiny space like a radio tuning all around me.

Click to click to click to click as tabs and panels jump up and about.

And I tab Fetty Wap. All quietly. Click. Who rose to prominence with his 2014 single 'Trap Queen', which was a sleeper hit that peaked at number two on the US Billboard Hot 100 chart. Click. And I like that song. A lot.

He sings a couple of lines of 'Trap Queen' by Fetty Wap.

And I tab. Tab Facebook *click* where Vin is being stalked by an unstoppable robotic assassin and Sam's watching cats and Kanye's bigger than rock and Lee wants '1 ov' I dunno what that is and we still can't find the llamas and Fetty Wap's vocals are vibrating through my mattress and my hips are rocking –

He sings a few more lines from 'Trap Queen'.

And I think about what you're doing right now...
And now.
And now.

And that every time I'm doing something... that so are you... that there's whole life... outside of me – life... this whole place where you've been present. Where I'm not.

And I want to be there...
Watching what you'd do.
Listening to what you'd say...

And I want you to touch me.
I miss your touch.

And your face feels so far away... and I need help... to get to you.

So I quickly, click, search for images… to help… to get me –
– to you…

And I google you because you're always here.
Close.

And the picture. And the headline.
NO.

And the number.
Fifth that year.

No.

Third at that particular.
NO.

I click away.

On to hot Jewish guys.
Click.
The IDF guy holds a prayer book, wears a dirty vest and tefillin.

But I click away because it…
Doesn't.

Stop.

And I click back on to Twitter and we're posting photos of dogs
protecting penguins and a tap tap *tap* tap tap on the door. Me
down. Screen down. Silence. Down. Shush.

Devorah's asking if I'm okay.

I'm fine I say.

Are you sure?

I don't want to tell her how much I –
You'd tell me?

MUM.

Because we're here if you –

Stop.

They're going out she says.
Will I be okay she says.
I will. I think I'll be alright.

Soon.

And off she goes.

And I count.

From ten.
And soon… before nine… I imagine you.

Like I do.

In the dark.

Blue-green eyes.
Messy hair. Cute smile.

Us two aliens. At either side of the Solar System… Venusian you. Ganymedian me. This little ET. Trying to call you home.

And I imagine you.
In tefillin… click.

Wrapped… all around your arms…
Holding you.

Taking you. Being taken…
And as I get into you. Really into…

PING. *You there?*

Weird… I was thinking about you…
Ping. *Be weirder if you weren't, no?*
Dunno…
Ping. *Why wouldn't we be in some kind of communicative sync that transcends all of space and time?*
You're so fucking clever I love you.

Ping. *You didn't come today.*

I'm sorry.

Ping. *You okay?*
Ping. *What you doing?*
Shabbat. You?

And I wait ages for your reply…

My heart beats in my mouth. Fast. Fast. Faster still. Waiting.
Where you gone?
Waiting. Again.
Fuck, have I upset you?
I read all of our messages back.

Twice.
Trying to find something I missed.

Twice.

Ping. *Sorry. Everyone's been here today.*
Ping. *Come Gants Hill*
I wish you could come to Hendon…
I don't say that. I do say.
It's ages
Ping. *It's like half an hour*
Gants Hill is the other side of London, Ad…
Ping. *I'm worth it…*
Yeah. Yeah you are.

My heart is racing as I sneak out.

I can't wait to see you.

Northern Line blur.

Bank. Blur.

Change.
Blur.

This is a Central Line train to Hainault via Newbury Park. The
next station is Stratford. Please mind the gap between the train
and the –

…lad on the other side of the carriage is kinda hot. He's older.
Maybe thirties… I've clocked him checking me out a couple of
times now. I think about fucking him. It's gone almost as
quickly as I think about it.
He smiles though. Nice.

Good arms.

I turn round to open the window thing. The mix of sweat, booze and curry is making me reel.

I pull out my phone. Nothing new on Facebook. Or Twitter.

So I open Grindr.

I never open Grindr. It's just something me and my mates do when we're fucking around... And a hundred profiles flash up all around me. I check mine.
It says I'm nineteen. It says I'm versatile. It says I'm cut.

Only some of this is true.

And then come the pings.
Badboi Online
Forty feet away

It's him. I flash a smile.

Ready. Aim...

You in to younger?

Yeah. He says.

How young?
Young young. He says.
He asks for pics. I tell him to go first.

Ping. Ping. Ping. Ping. Ping.

He's got a pretty decent dick on him and it goes on like that... the 'cock flurry' this... the 'wanna fuck me' that. This picture's not mine but he doesn't know. I cast and he bites and then I step off the Tube.

I close the app.

Think about you.

Delete the app

And head to the park clock.
Our spot.

And I'm smiling. I can hear my heart thump-a-thumping across my chest and echoing around my body.

I reach into the inside pocket of my jacket and notice my mini-*Zohar* is gone. My kippah is there though. The oversized knitted one Aunt Ada made for me. It's so ugly and big and obvious and white and urgh and I put it on ready to do my impression of Dungeon Master Rabbi Bloome cos that always makes you –

Dungeon Master's the educational lead on Jew camp and he's not anywhere as clever as he thinks and the fucker got us booted off and he's round with a funny walk and I start practising the walk and I'm immediately, firstly, kinda primarily aware of the matched pace.

Then in peripheral I count three.
I pull myself upright. Knee-jerk as much as anything… cos there's something about the intensity. The pace.

I speed up.
So do they.

I turn towards the park.
So do they.

And I'm suddenly really scared for like a laundry list of reasons, I'm afraid of them because well basic maths and and and I am entirely aware, like fully engaged with all the ways that they could hurt me, and I know that regardless of how hard I could fight back, bottom line – they're a group, they're a three.
A triad
A troika

A a a a triumvirate

A triptych

A fucking trinity and that makes me laugh a bit but doesn't really hide the fact that words may well form and clash and jump around my head but they don't quite silence that underlying rumble… three equals the upper hand and if they start I'm fucked.

I cross on to Valentines Park.
So do they.

I have one hand in my pocket fumbling around for something that I could use to defend myself because these numbers do not pan out for me. The key goes between the first and second fingers of my clenched fist.

And then I remember the kippah.
I pull out my phone. Message you. Let me know it's not just me…

I'm nearly here.

Click Facebook
Olive has made a giraffe, Buzlie links to a bunch of randoms who've crushed it and I forgot to wish Vin Happy Birthday.

I'm wearing the fucking kippah.

I click…

What you looking at?

Stop.

One on each side.
The other in front.

A triangle.

Slow, Dough and Ho.

I dunno why I call them that… Partly I guess to undermine them… Partly to steady the rising anxiety tightening across my chest… Partly cos Slow looks special, Dough's a bit fat and Ho's wearing too much make-up.

I feel like I'm standing tall but I slightly buckle

Just off to see a friend. Stammer it out…

Ho says she likes my little hat.

It's not that little actually.
I don't say that.

I do say thanks. And I move my hand up to take it away, start to walk on, but Dough has snatched it…

Panic rises.

And he's put it on wrong – like at the front… cock… *that's not how you wear it, you fat fuck…* and he is doing like this really shit German accent… asking Ho and Slow if the Yid-Lid suits him…

Fury rises.

They laugh. I shake.

My hands are back on the keys...
My entire body tenses...
I want to go apeshit
But I quietly ask for it back please

Shame rises.

Dough chucks to Slow and I try to swipe
Dough pushes me back
Slow catches... Shame rises.

Slow puts it on.

Something about looking like a dirty little Jew bitch
And I try to take it but he chucks it to Ho.

And I take a step forward but Dough pushes me back...

And she chucks it back to Slow.

And he stands there sneering at me.

And my shame rises panic rises and my vision swims...

He pulls out his lighter.
And he tries to set it on fire...

My whole everything immediately reels and I think I hear the
word Heeb... and something about an oven and and

And the red that I see. The entrancing, vivid, all-encompassing,
devastating, overwhelming, humbling profoundly vivid red that's
completely overtaken my line of vision, that's flooded my brain
and my throat and chest and my arms and my fists and my fists
explodes all around me and before he can react I am all over him.

My first punch breaks Slow's nose.
My second takes him out.

And my rage and my fury and all my my ferocity just detonate
and I try to calm and I try to imagine you but I swing round as
Dough punches me in the back of the head and –

Click.

Nothing as I hit the ground and Ho kicks into me

I try to imagine…

Click.

Tefillin

And I grab Dough's foot and pull

Click

Nothing as I manage to roll out of Ho's way and Dough tumbles

Click.

And I pull myself up and the real rage, the you rage in me builds and I want to fucking kill him.

And with each kick… as I remind him what a little fucking bitch he is

I think of you…
How you'd never let these morons anywhere near me.

I think of you…
How you'd leap to my defence if you were here…

You.
Umismali Gavri'el …
You.

Of the the the last time I saw you…

Skinny grey jeans.
Woolly hat.

Both heading home for Shabbat, both sad that we can't light candles together.

Yet. You say.

And I dunno what happens, I don't remember how but we go from nought to ninety in about two seconds flat as I spark at some lame-arse comment about *Sex and the City*, and before you know it we're screaming in the street.

Screaming.

And you're trying to make a point but I'm talking over you.
So you try again.
I block.
And again.
Block.
Can I go on
Is it a useful comment?
Well I don't know because you won't let me make it.
And on and round and up and down...

And then it erupts.

You do. Suddenly.

Yell me in my face to shut the fuck up.
SHUT.
THE.
FUCK.
UP.

And I lose it.

Oh my god, do I...

And it suddenly feels all so lost and awful, so suddenly lost and wasted, I mean, oh-my-god.
In less than five minutes.

And I can't remember what I've said but it basically amounts to fuck you, really to fuck you...

And you're upset, because we've never fought like this before.
I've never had a go at you before.

But it's because I'm upset too.
And I can't handle being this upset. Not with you.

And I still don't quite know how how how how

I can't even think as you go raging off on your bike.

No one fucking speaks to you like that...
And you circle back.

Demanding to know who the fuck I think I am?

And that look in your eyes as you shake your head.

And that sudden and complete disconnect as you ride off...

Just –

Just.

I call and call and I call and I call.
And I message and I Facebook and I call and I call.
And you ignore me.
Over and over and over again.
And shames rises.
Panic. When your phone shuts off.

Panic.
When I get the call two hours later...

Row after row after row of searing white fluorescent strips beat
down and rinse out the sickly pinks and greens of the hospital
waiting room whilst bleached disinfectal pungency mask vomit
and god knows what else.

It's supposed to be a vaguely decent hospital this one but I guess
all A&E departments orbit at least one of the Nine Circles of Hell.

Devorah paces back and forth and the constant a-clacking is
like scratched nails across a chalkboard.

Jesse tells her to sit down.
She does.
She's worried.
Wants you to be okay.
She's sure you are.
Yeah.

I say.

Yeah
Half-convinced.

Head goes into hands as I lean forward and try to hide into my
lap. Try to scrunch myself up into the smallest possible me and
tuck myself away.
And I push.
Further.

Smaller. Smaller. Smaller still but before I even get the chance to
go on, the door swings open and I just know it's going to be good.

And I stretch out and as my eyes adjust to the light as I take in
those same eyes and those thin lips and that kink in the hair of
of of of of –
– of this person of this woman that isn't –

You.

And you're all I can think about. *You.*

The day after.
You.
The day after when Jews –
All I can think about. *You*
And I'm at home beacause I couldn't…
You. What I did to you.

I've been staring at this wall for like five hours.
We have really shitty wallpaper.
My parents have like zero taste.
And I don't even clock Reuben in the room.
I have no idea why he's here.
NoideaIjustthinkaboutyou.
Or how long he's been watching.
I'm vaguely aware of the *C'mon, son.*
Vaguely with it as he takes me up to my room.
Ijustthinkaboutyou.
Cling to him as he tells me to let go. That it's okay to let go.

So I let go.
And sob into him.
Into dickhead Reuben like I've never sobbed

Dickhead Reuben. Never sobbed.
Stand over Dough like I've never sobbed, and I want to kick the
fucking shit out of him. I want to smash in the fat Anti-Semitic
motherfucker's face until there's nothing left of it as pain and
shame burn red-hot rivers of tears down my face...

Want to –

No no no no no no no...

That doesn't happen.
That doesn't...

              Doesn't.

I have to see you.

I have to.
Have to.

Run.

Out into space.
Us two little extra-terrestrials on either side of the Solar System...

Run.

Me. Ganymede.
The largest moon of Jupiter and the Solar System, and the only
moon known to have a magnetosphere.

The seventh satellite and third Galilean moon outward from
Jupiter.

Completing an orbit in roughly seven days, Ganymede shares a
one-two-four orbital resonance with Europa and Io.

A million kilometres from Jupiter.
And run.

Venus has no natural satellite.

And orbits the sun.
Alone.

At 108,000,000 km.
Run.

I could orbit you… There's enough room.

I hear them behind me and with each yell as they gain ground
and I run away from them and the pain and the shame and the
anger and the hate just.
Rises.

Ijustthinkaboutyou.

Orbiting you.
Like.
ET phone home.

And as as as as heart beats in my mouth beats in my lungs beats
in my throat beats adrenalin 'cross my chest and tension in my
arms shivers down across my back as my legs turn to jelly…

Because I have to get to you.
I have to talk to you.
I have to be with you.
And as I run at the wall of the cemetery I'm convinced I can
clear it.

And it doesn't take long to find you.

And as I curl down next to you memories and calls and chats
and joints and texts and tweets and love and mushrooms and
sex and cider and Sophie and Hebrew and politics and food and
crusades and pics and wine and fun and and movies and and
and and and some of it real and some of it not just
Stop.

Your bike. Crushed. Against the –

STOP

The timing of the stone-setting.
Can.

Can vary from community to community. In Israel, it's usually
at the end of the first month, but here… in Britain we do it at

the end of the year, to coincide with the first –
First anni–

I'm sorry I couldn't come today.

In in in in the Ashkenazi tradition the stone. The stone is left
upright at the head of the grave, but the Sephardim –
We lay them horizontally.

I rest my head against the newly laid headstone. And I tell you
that I never washed your T-shirt.

I don't know why that occurs to me.

The one I slept in the first time I ever stayed over.
That I've had it more than a year. That I stole it from your
bedroom.
That I sleep in it every night.

And I swear it stinks.

But it stinks of you and it stinks of me because it stinks of us
and I don't want to stop talking because I'm scared if I do the
conversation will be over this time so I want to keep talking so
it's like we're in bed and you're waiting patiently for me to
finish because you don't want to interrupt but I I I don't have
long because –
I hear them again. In the distance.

Fucking losers.
In triplicate.

Heading straight at me.

And I don't want them to find us.

And I don't want to fight.

I just don't have the energy.

I don't have the –

Run.
Try to avoid them as they gain as they gain.
Run.

Through graves and memorial, memories and pain
Run.
Run run run run run RUN at the cemetery wall.

But this time run I don't quite make it...
This time I don't clear the wall.

Just run.

This time I lose my footing.

I run.

And fall.
And run.

With such sheer force that I hurtle through space.

Fall

Past a hundred million tiny stars.

Run.
Past Venus.

And fall.
And Jupiter.

Run.
In their serene, expansive, orbital dance

Since the start of this month, Jupiter and and and all the stars
behind it have gradually slipped lower and lower and lower into
the evening twilight.

Whilst Venus hangs high.

And fall.
Run.
And fall.
Run.
And fall...

Into my orbital dance with you.

As the two brightest planets in the sky shift and circle as they
come close close closer still.

The God of Love and the God of Thunder conjunct to form
a luminous double star that lights up the night sky.

Run.

Merging as one, to the left of the moon.

Umismali Gavri'el ...

And as they do.

Must must run.

I notice how... how flawless Venus' orbit is.

With an eccentricity of less than nought-point-nought-one, an
almost perfect circle.

A Nick Hern Book

This revised edition of *Run* first published in Great Britain in 2017 as a paperback original by Nick Hern Books Limited, The Glasshouse, 49a Goldhawk Road, London W12 8QP

First published by Nick Hern Books in *Plays from VAULT* in 2016

Cover image: Richard Lakos

Designed and typeset by Nick Hern Books, London
Printed and bound in Great Britain by Mimeo Ltd, Huntingdon, Cambridgeshire PE29 6XX

A CIP catalogue record for this book is available from the British Library

ISBN 978 1 84842 661 0

www.nickhernbooks.co.uk

facebook.com/nickhernbooks

twitter.com/nickhernbooks